The Composer Steps into the Fire

by

Joseph Kerschbaum

With illustrations
by Nicole Yalowitz

1663 Liberty Drive, Suite 200
Bloomington, Indiana 47403
(800) 839-8640
www.AuthorHouse.com

© 2004 Joseph Kerschbaum
All Rights Reserved.

No part of this book may be reproduced, stored in a retrieval system, or transmitted by any means without the written permission of the author.

First published by AuthorHouse 08/23/04

ISBN: 1-4184-8902-6 (e)
ISBN: 1-4184-8903-4 (sc)

Printed in the United States of America
Bloomington, Indiana

This book is printed on acid-free paper.

Also by Joseph Kerschbaum:

The Human Remains (2002)
1 of 29 (2003)

Table of Contents

my mouth is full of winter

excavation	3
winter flowers	4
in the trees	5
feed us	7
we touch like cripples	8
kite flying	10
singing in waves	12
the doorway, exit ramp, i am not	13
jars	14
the composer steps into the fire	15

most of her transformation was mine

still waiting	21
porcelain thunder	23
visiting hours	24
casting shadows under shadows	29
old dreams (new nightmares)	32
monster	34
the sound of poisons	35
how i lost my arm	37

every night ends like this – with the broken neck of at least one of us

fractures	43
you can sleep in my mouth	44
foreign devils	46
last room rented	47
the sound of ice/the absent trails of angels	49

vii

sleeping in a room with a dead mouse	51
soil heart	52
a box of maniacs	56
ready were the almanacs	57
exiting her	59
you're all over the floor	60
map	62
striking matches underwater	65

I lie down in a papier-mâché museum that surrenders its artifacts for a new history

catacombs	73
marble shark teeth	74
how i am (1 of 29)	76
war of the worlds	78
culling song	81
hardware saint	84
it's not in me	85
shortening of days	88
drowning the ocean	89
balancing cracked scales	90
men of the cloth	92
how sorry he is	93
replacing our bodies	95
autumnal equinox	97
aftermath	98

my mouth is full of winter

excavation

He materializes in the morning
after a night of canyon excavations
where all of the stars
descend like attainable dreams
to the core of the Earth.
He is learning to navigate
the tunnels beneath the surface
as if learning to breathe
with his whole body.

Every night he finds all new hollows
inside himself waiting
for cave paintings, remnants of warm fires,
jewelry made of elephant tusks.
Here, down in the bowels of his essence,
reside the stars, tablatures,
and all the artifacts she buries
within him.

winter flowers

My mouth is full of winter.
Spring surrounds me like hungry flies.
I offer flowers at the ends of my fingers.

I would speak but my lips have blisters.
Like any infection, my words need sterilized.
My mouth is full of winter.

When we embrace we leave only splinters.
Every injury, I have memorized.
I offer flowers at the ends of my fingers.

Every year, every season slips by faster.
I measure distance with my heart – not my eyes.
My mouth is full of winter.

This hemisphere of mistakes will be perfect after
everything has been revised.
I offer flowers at the ends of my fingers.

No one stays in this season, they're all visitors.
They drop from my hands like suicides.
My mouth is full of winter.
I offer flowers at the ends of my fingers.

in the trees

The wind isn't innocent anymore –
she uses it as an instrument.
The sky outside this window darkens
as she composes unwelcome nocturnes.
In the vacancies between days
she plays instruments with broken strings
in a winter orchestra
only I can hear.
Her bones are strung up
in the empty trees around my house.
She gives tone, rhythm to the wind
as she taps against the branches
and the trunks of the trees
all night and all day –
a minstrel
who has nowhere else to go.

feed us

We stand in rows,
trees in an orchard.
Arms out stretched
to catch as much sun
as possible. We hold our hands
to the sky. We extend our arms
in life, the bearing of life,
the birth of the granted –
the fathers and mothers
of the unconsumed.
When the first frost stiffens our limbs
we drop our children
to the earth.
The ground is littered
with our children, wrapped
in sweetness, sticky
on the lips.
Most of them will rot.

We wait for the fire that will burn us
down to ashes. So few of us burn.
Every winter, as if
we have never been stripped bare before,
the tree next to me says,
I always thought we would be
more beautiful than this.

we touch like cripples

(The arms are dull butter knives. Rounded at the ends

like baseball bats. No hands: unable to cling,

to grasp with urgency. Able to embrace

but don't. No fingers mean no music can be played. Opening doors

is extracting confessions from the innocent. Hard-fought, meaningless.

Shame is elicited from breathing. Stay at arms length

like careful doctors. The arms, trying to carve braille

into the foreheads of blind women. The deaf

can't hear car bombs removing the faces of buildings

or the hum of bees. With no one speaking

is there a difference? The handless long for sign language.

Arms waving, trying to signal passing ships that aren't there.)

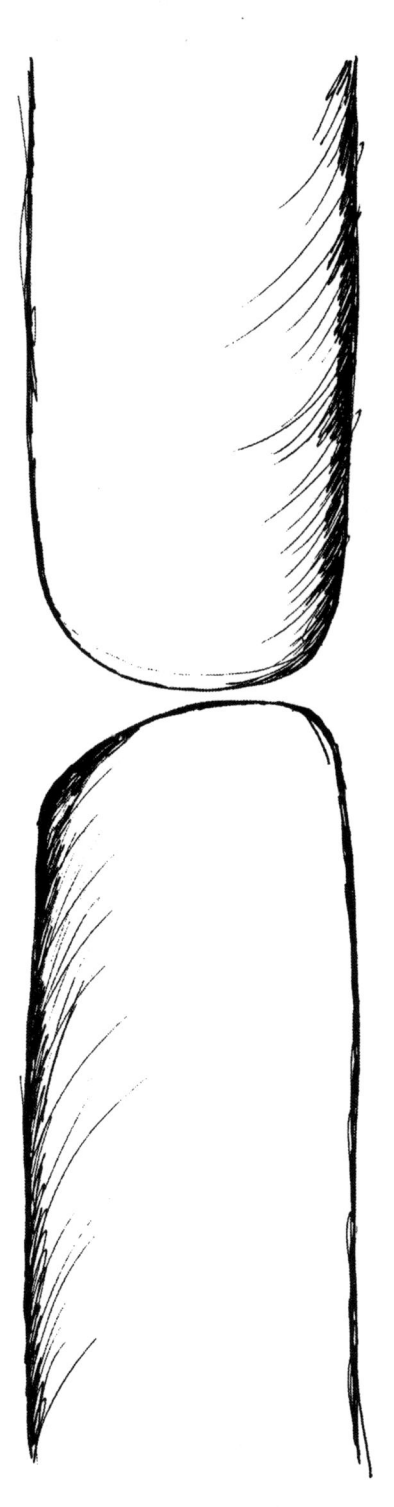

kite flying

The sky was so blue
that it wasn't blue
any longer. The sky ascended our spectrum
and forged it's own definition of blue.
Every time that sky
comes back into my mind
the colors shift, the blue
gets bluer and the horizon widens.
The ink spot in that new blue sky
was my kite as I raised it
higher into the atmosphere. I felt
like I was riding the wind
and disappearing into the new blue distance
but my feet were hard on the ground.
When I was a child
this was my favorite way
to spend an afternoon.

The last time I flew a kite,
the time when blue wasn't the ocean,
it wasn't a mood, it wasn't rain clouds,
and it wasn't the sky –
this blue was all of them.
Or maybe I was all of them
and the sky was just the sky.
My kite was as high as the string
would let it go. My feet
were walking on a world
no longer my own.
The last time I flew a kite
I wasn't flying a kite.

As my kite rose higher,
color splashed
into my black-and-white life.
Standing in the middle of an open field
with the wind in my face
I lost myself and just for a minute
I lost your absence.
You were still gone –
you just weren't on my mind.
Finally, I could breathe
and my mouth didn't have your aftertaste.
That blue wasn't the ocean,
a mood, a rain cloud,
or the sky but it had nothing
to do with your death –
it only had to do with me
at least for that first moment.

As my kite continued to rise
into that impossible blue
I thought about
how we never flew kites
together.

singing in waves

The longer the season stays,
the more her fingers resemble branches.
Leafless, bare branches grasp
for the frozen sky. Cloudless, the sky
empty like her mouth. Abandoned,
her mouth is a cave. Caves are holes
waiting to become homes or tombs
coated in ice. Her tongue is a sheet of ice.
Slippery surfaces lick the bottoms of feet
trying to maintain their balance.
Her feet, immobile as tongues
stuck to frozen pipes. Unable
to walk into flames or arms,
her feet are useless as dead salmon. Her heart,
like salmon, waits to be lured, gutted, explored.
Not gutted like winter – void of warmth,
breath. Void of a gravitational center –
cold moon dreams of being a satellite,
of singing in waves.

the doorway, exit ramp, i am not

The name in the newspaper
belongs to the father of a childhood friend and I haven't
thought of that boy or his father in years because I lost
touch with their family when I was 11, but I remember
the young boy who wanted to be like his father,
the police officer whose name was in the newspaper
after he took his own life with his service revolver.
I will never see Rob Sr. again but I remember him
as a large, gentle man who owned exotic birds
but perhaps by chance I will run into his son,
Rob Jr., my childhood friend, and I won't know
what to say to him so I will avert
my glance, not make eye
contact, get out of the store
aisle or off that sidewalk
as quickly as possible because I won't
want to be infected with his misery because I already can't stop
thinking about his father, the stitches that unraveled
to the point where his life fell down around his ankles;
I don't know the details of his father's failures,
but perhaps that would be what my friend
from my childhood needs: someone
removed from the situation so that he can escape his father,
forget the mold that he has so willingly cast himself.
He could slip into his childhood, just for a minute,
and I could be that element, that brief exit ramp, but I won't
because I'll be ducking out of sight.

jars

In the cooling evenings the sky
came alive with lights.
We trapped them.
We swung our jars
through the air
harvesting stars
to take home.

We watched those jars shine
as if we had captured God's tears.
Those lights never lasted long
in jars with no slits at the tops.
We never suspected
those tiny deaths
were our doing.

The cinders that resided in the air
burnt out or went away
or perhaps we caught them all.
Now, the air is thin with what is here
and thick with what is missing.

the composer steps into the fire

Your mouth blooms like a fresh bruise.
Even your blood, pressed against your skin
like a face against smeared glass, is looking for a way out.
All you have to do is step through the burning
circular doorway. You won't be exiting or entering.

The movement under his fingers is ripe.
Each touch leaves blisters. Now
your old garments have been rendered
useless, he can dress you
with his lips, teeth, and his tongue.

Silence turns into an orchestra of your swelling nerves.
They light up like the brightest CAT scan.
The forest of your body is set ablaze.
Your skin is brush burned away.
Your body is a ravished prairie.

He puts his torches away and watches you
reflect against the night sky like a distant city
beyond the dark horizon. You can be seen for miles.
As the stars become one inside your illumination,
the composer steps into the fire.

*most of her transformation
was mine*

still waiting

He told her

    about what he did.

He was

    breathing too hard

to finish his sentences.

    She patted his shoulder

and she spoke

    in concerned tones.

He crushed his eyes

    closed and waited

for warm words.

    He gave his mother the details

of the bad thing he did.

    She told him

he shouldn't have.

    He asked her

if he would

    still get into heaven.

She said

    that would be up to God.

porcelain thunder

If clouds were made of glass
this is how they would sound.

Crashing into each other,
crumbling down into soapy water.

The storm of her fury rushed through the house
like the sound of distant violence. The clattering

of dishes, the slamming of cabinets,
the stomping of feet

rattled the windows like garbage trucks
when they drove by.

I found shelter in my room upstairs.
Like the storms outside, these storms were void of reason.

Unlike the storms outside, the horizon
didn't darken with foreshadowing –

the world just erupted.
As the evening lengthened

I dissected myself to reveal what I did
to change her to a tornado.

The porcelain thunder resonated till I fell asleep,
still hiding in my bedroom.

In the morning I woke to silence
and breakfast and a clean kitchen.

visiting hours

...I don't
know
what else
to say.
I think
you've stopped
listening.
Drifting
off
like a ship
not tied to
the dock.
Lost in
the harbor.

I ask
the nurse
to bring
more
juice.
I ask
her
when your
next dose
will be
administered.

She says
she's not sure.
Probably
the day after
next.
As the nurse
sets the dinner
down
you say
you can't
eat it.
The nurse says
depletion
of the appetite
is normal
toward the end
of the chemo
cycle.
I nibble at
the neglected
food
on the
silver tray.
The food
tastes

cool, metallic
but it keeps
my hands
and mouth
busy.

I chew
slowly.

I don't
know what
else to do.
I try
to drudge up
any other details
of my day
to fill this
numb, heavily
medicated
space between us –
nothing arrives.

All we have
is this –
these white
walls.

If you
aren't
going
to be
here,
I wish
you
wouldn't
be here
at all.

You are
a water-
color
painting
washing
away.
Your voice
is a gas
leak.

You say
you want to
walk around.
Your legs
don't have
the strength
to carry
your body.
Your mind
isn't present enough
to coordinate
the shuffling of feet.
I help you
keep your balance
with my hands
firm
on your shoulders.
I don't want
to touch
you. Your brittle
skin is moss
grown over
the arms
that once
embraced me.

You feel
like you
will break
apart
between
the hesitation
in my
hands.
I don't know
what else to do.
I do
what you ask
because
I can't think of
anything
except leaving.
I can't...

casting shadows *under shadows*

I'm killing myself
to kill you.
The more I waste away
the less there is for you
to consume.
The rivers of my veins
are polluted.
Death and life
have eroded inside me –
they are faceless twins.
I get them confused sometimes
so I refuse
both of their out stretched hands.
This is my station now –
between.

>*I will not stop*
>*until I've eaten*
>*your entire body.*
>*I am thousands of mouths*
>*feasting on your essence.*
>*I will chew*
>*through you*
>*until I am*
>*chewing on myself.*
>*Once only I remain*
>*we will be one*
>*in our breathlessness.*

My body is too weak
to extract me from this bed.
I fade into clean sheets
until I am a whitewashed shadow,
an indentation, that needs to be

checked on from time to time.
When the sun shines through the window,
or the lights are turned on,

I disappear. When the lights are shut off
I am free of this bed. I linger
in the darkness. I am
shadow boxing.
Not sure if I'm the shadow
or the boxer.

> *I will not ask you to dance –*
> *I will simply steal your feet*
> *and waltz you down*
> *below the grass*
> *where we*
> *will listen*
> *to the rain*
> *resounding*
> *like a round*
> *of applause.*

My skin will not be
the border of my civil war.
My skin will be
sweet to the touch
like a peach.
I will hear Moroccan music
playing and I will dance
with myself. Against
the crowd, the beat –
only with myself.
My skin will not be
just what I leave behind –
my skin will sing
even if I can't.

I will not stop
until I've eaten
your entire body.

I'm killing myself
to live. I inject poison
as if it were ambrosia.
I will kill my death –
resurrect my life.
Come summer
I will swim in my body.
I will shine brighter
and hotter than the sun.
My children will dance
as I cast their shadows
on the ground.

I will not stop   *I will not stop*
until my shadow   *until your shadow*
is mine.   *is mine.*

old dreams (new nightmares)

There were 15 years before
all this. They reside in black-and-white photographs
like dreams in poor-quality memories.
Unlike this surround-sound
digital nightmare.

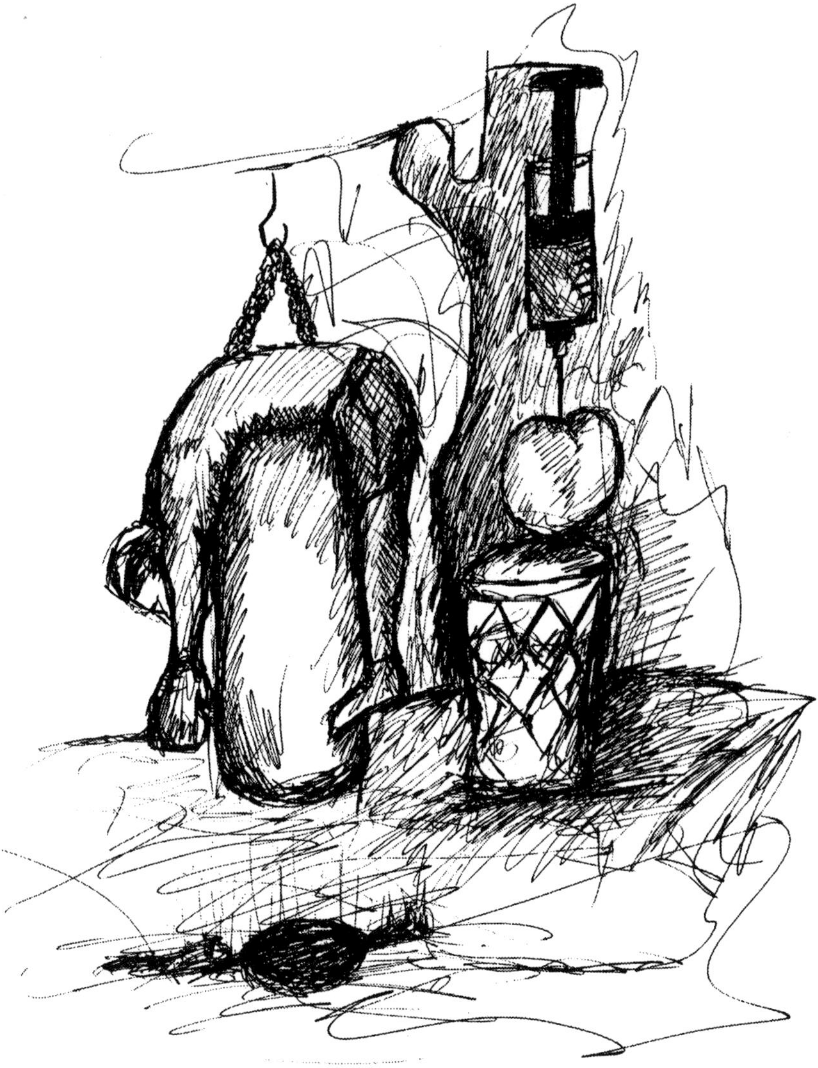

monster

She changed.
Not as much as I did.
Most of her transformation
was mine.
She still ended up
the monster.

the sound of poisons

If I could find you
I would ask you to dance.
We never had a chance to waltz
at a wedding reception
or an anniversary. Even if we did
I would have been too young to enjoy it –
I would be watching
everyone watching me
dance with this older lady.
All I would have thought about was
everyone else. Now
I can't even find your grave.

If I could find you
I would dig you up
and ask you to kiss me.
Lips cracked and chapped
when you died. They weren't
always that way. Pull you
from the ground.
Save you
the way I never could
when you were here.
The way I never tried.

If I could find you
I would dig you up
and ask what you thought
of me. Did your growing weaker
happen from my pulling away?
Is there anything you never did
that I could do in your place?
Is it true what they say
about the afterlife,

that your life before
is just an afterthought
once you're gone?

I already know the answers.
Like watching a movie
for the hundredth time,
still hopeful for a better ending.
Or at least a different one.
Today will end
with me folding this map,
driving home frustrated
at my lack of a sense of direction.

If I could find you
I would leave you
where you are. I would put
a ceramic bowl on your grave
to catch the rain
just in case you got thirsty.

how i lost my arm

The world has been burnt down
in a conflagration sparked
by my teeth. Night after night
it dwindled from an inferno down to a match head
burning my fingertips. In desperation
I tossed a rotted tree onto it. I learned quickly
the world around me was ripe
with fuel, the world rendered to splinters and ashes.
The first night after I fed my house to the fire
I stood naked and watched the stars soar past.
I am not sure how many nights have passed like this
but I know I have not slept indoors for years.
Fire has no mouth, but it swallows everything –
the world just isn't enough to keep it going.
At my feet the fire pleaded like a death row inmate
for me to grant this memory a stay of execution.
With nothing left to fuel this fire,
I stuck my hand into the flames.
My flesh slowly burned away. My ashes dissolved
like stars in the morning sun. Unlike stars,
my ashes would not return the next night.
I know this fire is my memory, and everything I feed to it
I feed to myself. My hand is now a fist of bones –
what happens when I have no flesh left to burn?
Does this memory just smolder to cinders, to ashes?
Does the wind blow me away? Will I exist
after I have consumed my body?
My entire arm is gone now and the fire is
on its death bed. Preparing to shove my other arm
down this fire's throat, I hesitate.
The fire grows cold, a scar on the ground.
My ashes swirl around me like fireflies.
I open my mouth and swallow them.
With my black tongue, I kiss the sun.

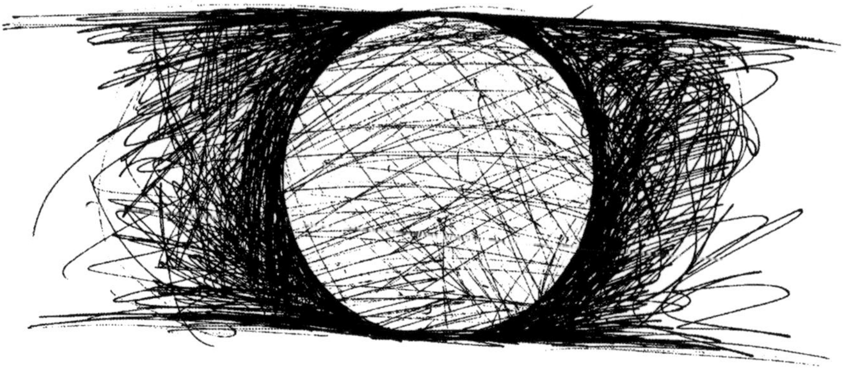

every night ends like this —
with the broken neck
of at least
one of us

fractures
(after 4 boys drowned on Dec. 17, 2002 in Minnesota)

      A hairline fracture
           opens   and swallows
                 the boys.

      Like a child gasping
         during an asthma attack,
the frozen mouth sucks in what life it can.
         The boys are inhaled
    as quietly as naked branches
                 shaking in no wind.

The incident happens so suddenly
                          it almost doesn't

    happen.

        Slow freezing is peaceful.
            The auditorium of the lungs fills
    with no applause but the open mouths
of a shocked audience
            who can't accept

    how quickly
        and quietly
the end comes.

you can sleep in my mouth

When you run,
and you will run,
my arms will be
the fallout shelter
where the little demons of this world
won't fool or harm you.
Year after year you are driven
from the places you haunt,
your forests and houses.
You flee likes refugees from a war
that is never started or finished.
The little witches, devils, and angels
find you unsuspecting, never learning.
You run from them like children from lightning.
Run to me.
You can sleep in my mouth.

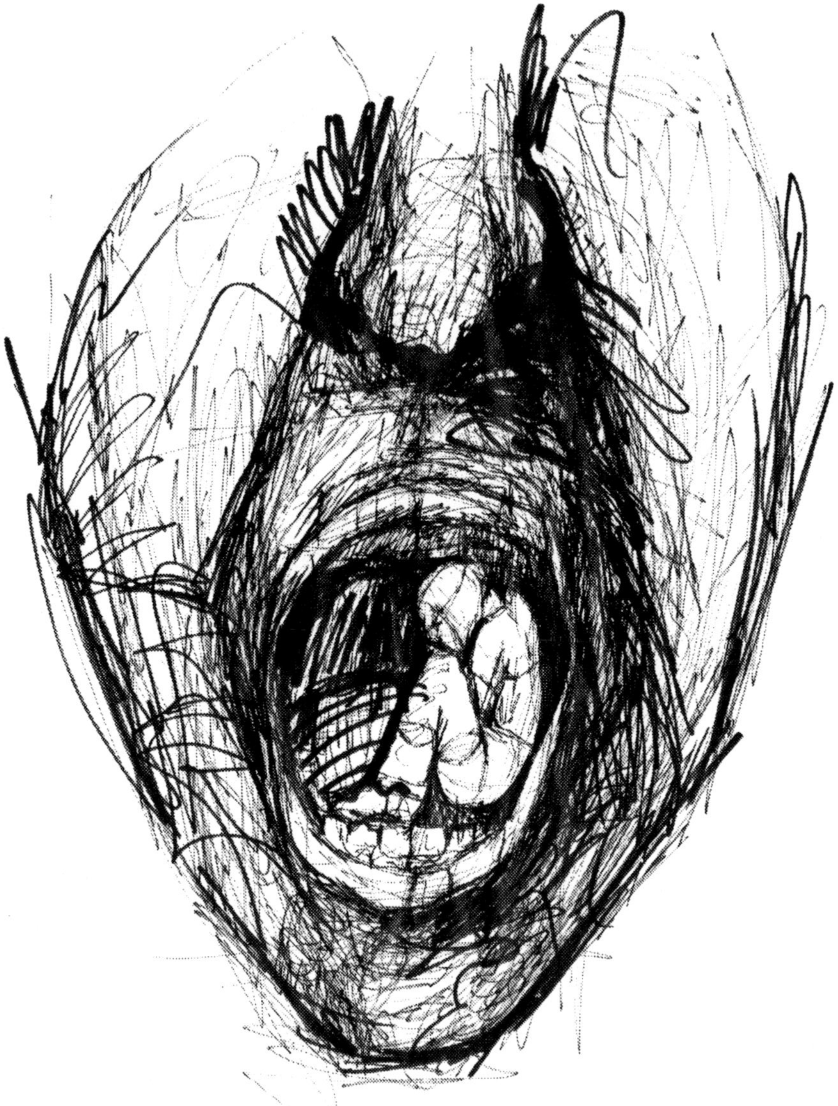

foreign devils

They enter the crowd fresh
from the depths of hell.
Their arrival isn't noticed.
The streets are already populated
with demons and other creatures
of the underworld. The stories and myths
told to them are sadly based on fiction.
Nothing left here but their kind.
The living evacuated long ago.
No souls, sweet like candy, left to taste.
They leave knowing hell
and Earth are parallel.

last room rented

If you look close enough
you can still see the rope burn

around the rafter in the center of the room.
When the television turns off

you can hear his toes skimming the floor
like a ballerina only wishes hers could.

At 10:30 in the morning the electricity shuts off
for a split second. This is the minute his necked snapped –

the minute this room became a setting for a story.
If you ask the motel staff about room 16

they spin this yarn
of how this room is haunted

and how all these things are true. They rent out this room
only when the whole place is booked.

The apparition turns on the hot water,
turns off the lights, and sleeps next to you in the bed.

They say you can hear him breathing in your ear.
This has to be untrue because that apparition

would never sleep with you or anyone in that bed.
He never could sleep with someone lying next to him –

even the women he loved.
He would listen to the rhythm of their breathing.

He would try to synchronize his heart
with theirs. He thought of how their hearts

would not beat together for long, then not at all.
With all these mice in his head, he couldn't sleep.

The power shouldn't shut off
at 10:30 because Tony died at 1 in the afternoon.

If you look close enough
you won't see a rope burn

around the center rafter
because he used an electrical cord.

The gentleman behind the counter
doesn't understand why I am asking to stay in this room

but he thought I should know about the ghost
that lives there. He doesn't necessarily believe

in all the ghost stories he's heard. But
he says that visitors find it interesting.

After he spins his yarn about the haunting
I give the key to the room back to him

and decide not to stay. Tony's body succumbs
to myths. His body turns into the dust leaping

through sunlight like wounded deer.
I am sleepless with dreams of his dreams.

The gentleman behind the counter is correct,
this was the last room rented.

the sound of ice/the absent trails of angels

i.

The wind has frozen itself still.
The hum of the streetlight is dull,
dominates the frozen air.
Cars are lined up like white elephants
on both sides of the street.
Silence constantly shatters
its own presence.
Only when we are removed
does the world achieve this level
of purity.

ii.

Asleep. This street is asleep.
I listen to the snow fall.
Sounds like quiet breaths –
like a body sleeping easy
with relief. Breaths long
like snow fall. Erasing
like snow fall. The night painted
white, halos around streetlights,
as if angels appear
only when snow falls.
When these angels depart,
they leave no tracks on the ground
so we can't follow them back
to wherever they come from.
There are other methods to find
their homes. I will stay,
listen to the city sleep –
accept the halos for what they are.

sleeping in a room with a dead mouse

A snap wakes
me. I am
not sure
I was
sleeping.
Perhaps I was
snapped
out of consciousness –
into sleep.
My head is
heavy with dreams
(or is it
heavy
with reality?).
I can't
lift it.
My ears
are full of
a language
I don't
understand.
My mouth
is full of
a language
I can't speak.
They are not
the same language.
We all know
shadows and temptation
lead to dark places
but we never learn.
Every night ends
like this –
with the broken neck
of at least
one of us.

soil heart

This morning has been coming for a long time.
Like the pain in my knee pounding away,
until my left leg is rendered useless,
I refrain from admitting the inevitable
until I am submerged in morning's cold new light
unable to lift my body off the dead soil.
This morning is the consequence I knew was waiting –
it is worse than I could have imagined.

I wake at 4:30 a.m.
My shower is not warm.
I come down the stairs, my knee
screaming, confessing the world.
If I take my leg to a doctor he will not
tell me anything that I don't already know.
My body is crumbling. He can't stop that
so I will save him the trouble.

The air outside is still thick with dreams.
Stepping out into the silence of the back field,
I know it is dead. My fingers have pulled
at its heart for years. This morning
the soil is a corpse.

Every morning my fingers break
the veins and roots under the ground.
The worms, crickets, night crawlers, and maggots
are my fruit. Before sunrise I come out
here, to my field to lift the life from the soil.
Plastic cups with plastic lids hold my treasures
like vaults. The fishermen come to my store
for their bait. They used to come to my store –
this morning will be the last of that.

The soil is void like I imagine space – just as black.
My fingers dig into the soil. All I find is soil.

No worms, maggots, or stars –
just dirt. Regions of my field have been
evacuated before but repopulated later.
This is different. They are gone.
Hours of digging turn up nothing.
The sky, overcast with souls
leaving the corpse of the earth.

I put my ear to the soil to listen
for anything. The ground is silent
like space above me. Crouching to the ground,
my knee finally revolts, I fall. I am covered in dirt.
My hands tremble from the chill. My teeth chatter.
I know my body has deteriorated for years,
and this is why I can't lift myself
from the ground –
but I can't help but feel
the soil is bending gravity, pulling me down,
trying to swallow me.
The Earth consumes people everyday:
we force its mouth open
and drop bodies down its throat.
I know the ground
isn't swallowing me
but I know it is.

The soil tastes dull as I swallow it.
My hands shovel dirt into my mouth
as if I could bring it back to life inside me.
As if I can fix this situation by reversing
our roles. I know I can't bury the soil
inside my body. So much evidence
I can't hide.

This morning has been coming for a long time.
Today the Earth enters me. Tomorrow
I will return to the Earth to confess
what I've done.

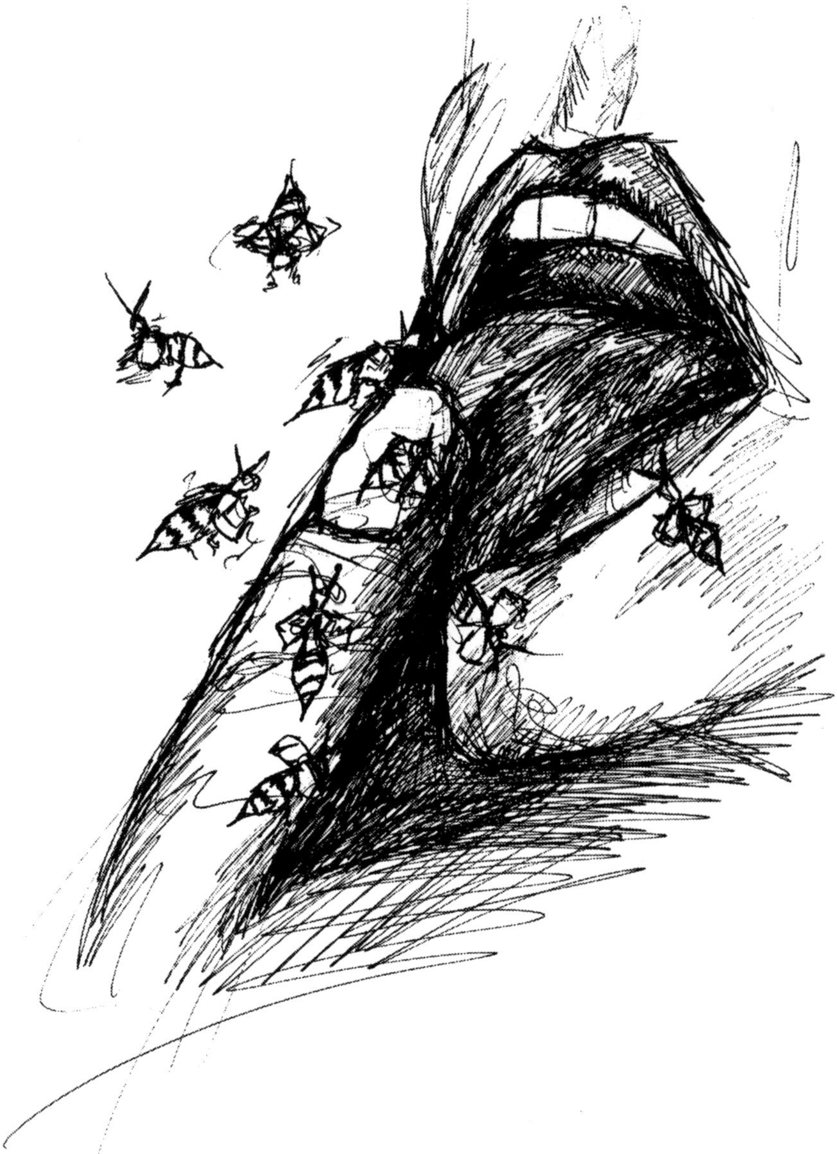

a box of maniacs

They hum like a distant mob lulling me into violence.
The heat of summer in their veins. Find blossoms inside me.
Thrashing against themselves, boxed in and senseless.

The box in the backyard came from a great distance.
In my dreams, I hear them in my sleep.
They hum like a distant mob lulling me into violence.

To leave myself simply wounded would be kindness.
Wood and skin contains violence unseen.
Thrashing against themselves, boxed in and senseless.

They flood the sky when they escape the surface.
Without them the air is hollow, no sense of urgency.
They hum like a distant mob lulling me into violence.

Their song is mine, sounds like my silence.
They sting the insides of my eyes.
Thrashing against themselves, boxed in and senseless.

They need out now. They won't live to see the next solstice.
Open the box/my mouth. Set them free.
They hum like a distant mob lulling me into violence.
Thrashing against themselves, boxed in and senseless.

ready were the almanacs

God constructed a valley for reaching.
The mountains were cool and always evening.

I will find you in this place.
I won't find all of you.

The wake of your walk was wide and dementing.
I caressed the sweetness of your undertow.

This improbable dawn yields
blossoms shocked into open mouths.

O please be more than gilded grist, my sweet.
I wagered my wrists on your sincerity.

Between our lips there is a fragile silence stirring —
the waiting for something greater than us.

Ready were the almanacs
to display how lost I was.

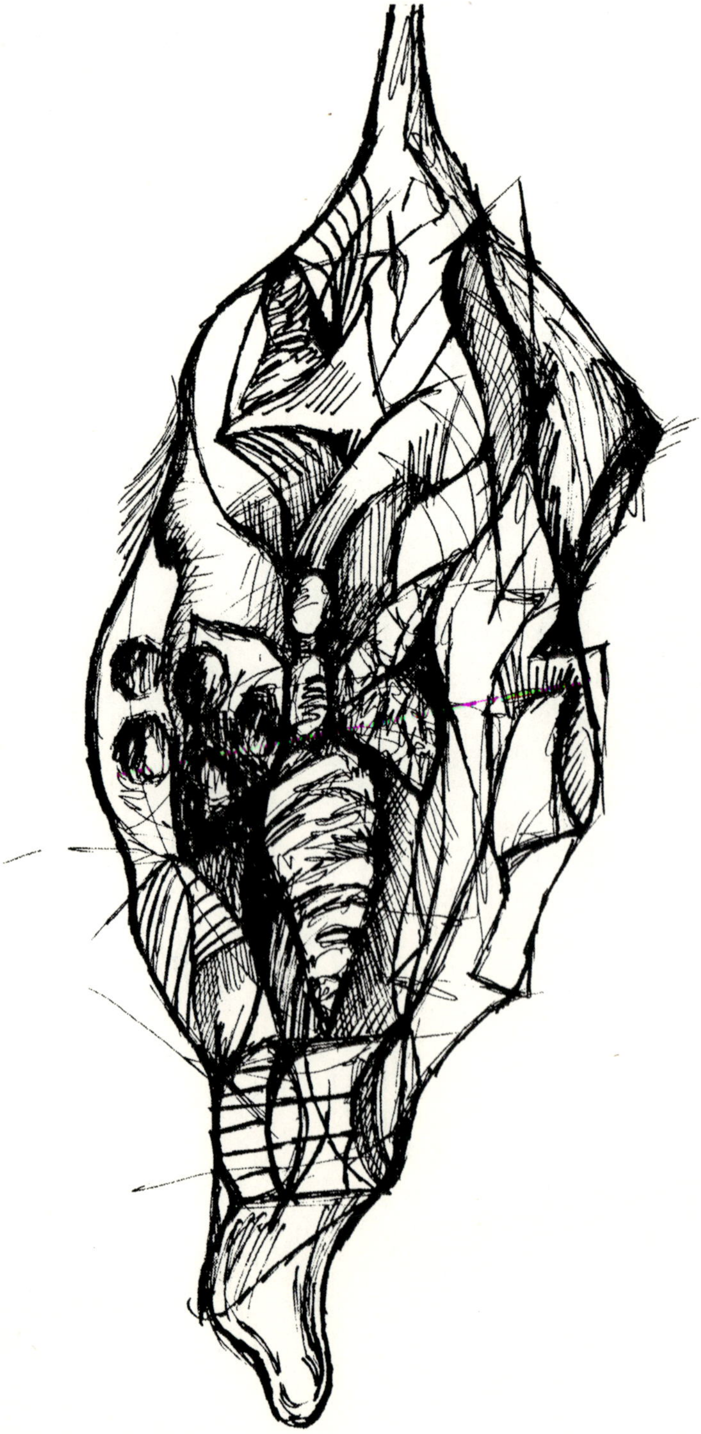

exiting her

       The only promise I kept
       is the wound I left
                       behind.
          I tried to please at least
          one of us
              tonight
but I broke. I spilled

              empty into the room.

                     I coated the walls,
             mingling with the darkness,
         looking for a way out.

        All I found was light
                in the next room   erasing me.

      Tonight was
               broken porcelain
      packed in a box
                 in the back of a closet.
In the dark, I dressed myself.

      I couldn't tell if it was my clothes or my skin

that didn't fit anymore.

you're all over the floor

Every corner of this house
has the deposits you've left
behind. You are woven into my couch. You clog
the drain in my bathroom sink.
Flakes of your skin and hair
wander around in the stale sunlight
like lost tourists. I inhale your exhaust.
The dust I'm leaving behind
will intertwine with your dust.
Our bodies will dance without us being in the room.
When the dancing settles down we will hide in corners,
under tables, like children hiding from
strangers. Eventually, we will be
discovered. We will be swept up and forgotten –
then we will be one
like we always should have been.

Snow

falling

leaves

me

with

nothing.

map

I'm leaving.

She left.

Leaving behind my life that isn't mine. My life
I never wanted in the first place. This place
isn't my life – but my death.
I'm leaving my death.

*She tried to leave her death behind like it's not instilled
in her bones. She couldn't just leave her death behind
like something she forgot to pack.*

This morning is my new birthday.
My flesh is not new today but
everything else is. I love my mother but this morning
my mother is not giving birth to me –
I am. The contractions are just me breathing
for the first time.
With each step, the misconceptions of myself
lose strength,
suffocating as I steal my own breath
like a cat inhaling the life of a sleeping infant.

*She just took off. The convictions of a stray dog.
Lost. We woke up to the new hollow that was our hearts.*

I carve myself out of myself as if my skin is a layer of ice.
I leave me behind. I take me with.
No one sees me leave because I don't.
As I walk away I stay.

*We wouldn't even recognize her now, it's been so long.
I wonder if she would recognize us: older, withered.
She must be a woman by now, was she a woman when she left?*

This morning I am still a virgin –
but I couldn't be more of a woman.
My body is completely mine.

How long has she been gone?

Years.

Years have passed.

The past is hollow.

How did she feel?

I feel like new glass.

*Like glass, my heart shattered when she left
but I doubt she's even thought of me.*

I don't look back much as a rule. Mistakes only grow larger
with distance, with time to give them substance.

*Years later I still hadn't heard from her.
No letters, no postcards, no phone calls.*

I leave my landlocked home, my heart.
I arrive at what should be the coast.

*If she had just asked, I would have told her so long ago
that whatever she left to find wouldn't be there.*

According to the map I found in the basement,
the ocean should be here. Right here.
I don't understand. Is the ocean just a myth?

It's all a myth.

Shells don't sound like the ocean –
they are just hollowed-out homes
filled with ghosts whispering, crying in waves.
I have to see this for myself.

She had to see for herself.
Would she listen if I had told her?

I won't listen.
I need to leave.

Would she still have left?

I'm so far away from home.

The ocean was just as missing when I left too.
I hope she wasn't sorry.

I'm sorry.

striking matches underwater

Her walking out
the door was
the wind being
knocked out
of my lungs,
the air being
sucked out of
this room.
Matches
would not
burn
when she was
gone.
When she was gone
flames were
a viable answer
to this shattered
equation
but I could not
get a strangled match
to spark.
I lacked
the ability
to live
or die.
Empty lungs
sucking on
hollow air
sound like
tires squealing
on blacktop.
After three
breathless days,
just as I was losing

my ability to do math,
she came back.

She came back
like Christ
but more like rain
to a scorched prairie.
My lungs in need
of saving,
in need
of oxygen,
which doesn't
just linger
in the air,
were born again.
Tonight, she is
in this room
like I need oxygen
to be in this room.
The breaths
I've taken in tonight
have not been just
filtered and processed,
but I've lived
each one of them.
Tonight she is
in this room —
she allows matches
the opportunity to burn
but I choose
to strike them
underwater.

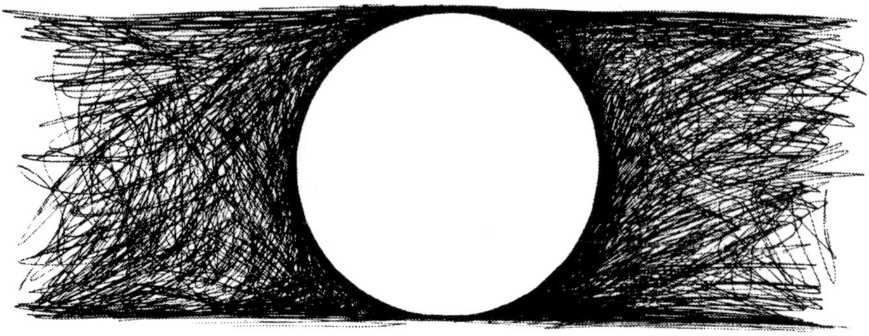

*I lie down in a papier-mâché museum
that surrenders its artifacts
for a new history*

catacombs

Entire cities are buried within me.
Every morning is a wake for the departed.
No one is missing entirely.
When I lie down I feel tombs shift under my skin.

Every morning is a wake for the departed.
They reside below the topsoil, inside my chest.
When I lie down I feel tombs shift under my skin.
Each year my catacombs deepen.

They reside below the topsoil, inside my chest.
I am cluttered as a Jewish graveyard.
Each year my catacombs deepen.
Each year another city turns to bone and disappears.

marble shark teeth

I keep the wheels spinning
as smoothly as I can
as if I am carrying a serving tray
stacked with tumblers filled
with the most exquisite liquor
ever extracted from wormwood.
I am carrying this tray at 70 mph
over wet pavement, trying
not to spill a drop
or even cause ripples
in these tiny oceans.

The highway
is a smoky piano bar at 3 a.m.
The regulars look at my car
as if it's a foreigner – and it is.
I drive in silence, in darkness.
The vacuum of my senses
conjures images out of darkness
as if it were made of marble.
Like sharks in dark water,
these memories wait until
I am floating peacefully.

I find every memory I've abandoned
wandering the shoulders of dark highways.
Headlights flash against them like deer
standing, waiting to cross.

She is asleep in the back seat.
A change of direction (like an exit ramp)
or a change of speed (like a traffic jam)
will pull her awake.
My white-knuckled hands are firm

on the ridges of the wheel.
My eyes, red veined and fatigued, focus
on the white line in the center of the road
flashing in and out of sight.
I keep my distance from everyone
so that the wake of their travel
will not disturb her sleep. Just sit here
and drive with this inhabited darkness
tapping on the windshield. It wants in.
It is in.

She doesn't need any of this.
I sustain her dreams
the best I can.

how i am (1 of 29)

This cafe usually isn't this busy on a Thursday evening but tonight
every table is taken. At the table next to me, a woman with blonde hair,
small hands, and a small smile picks up her bag
and leaves. As she rises out of her seat a man places his bag
on the table staking his claim on the valuable space
just released. The man sets his large, blue backpack on the table,
looks around, and walks out. As I stare at the bag I wonder
what this man is studying, where is he from, and does he smoke?
I can see him through the window. He's not smoking. He's looking
around and talking on a cell phone – then he hangs up. Why
did he leave his bag here? Possibly to save his seat?
This is a busy place. Someone could steal his bag. Or maybe
there is something in that bag he doesn't want. Just yesterday
a bomb detonated in Bali and killed 180 people in a cafe
much like this one. That sort of thing happens
all over the world now. Why can't it happen in Indiana? The man
is still outside. He had a dark complexion and could be
of Middle Eastern descent. Not that I think everyone
with a dark complexion is a terrorist but why did this guy drop off
a large bag and walk out? Should I say something? Would I be a racial
profiler? Do I suffer from media-poisoning? Have I been so changed
by what I've seen recently that anyone who leaves a bag on a table
is ready to make a statement and claim lives?
And where did that guy go? I should say something
to him. He should know that these are sensitive times,
and one should consider one's actions more closely. He
might take offense but he has to know, and I'm ready to be
on the offensive should he become defensive. In fact,
I hope he becomes defensive because I want to drive my point
home to this prick. If he isn't a terrorist – then I will teach him
a lesson. If he is a terrorist – then I'll never see my father again. I'll
never able to ask him about Vietnam and the smell of a morning
you thought you'd never see. My niece needs help

but she won't be able to get it from me. With one tick I will become the smudge on the family history. I will serve as a springboard into nostalgia, better days that haven't been that good. When this bomb goes off I'll be "1 of 29 dead" in the newspaper and I'll be a victim of the bigger picture – the world picture. The last picture
I'll have is this bag as it scatters me all over and ends me. Should someone's passing be so sorrowful and full of rage? I thought it was supposed to be peaceful and warm. And the warm air from outside brushes my face as the man sits down at his seat with a cup of coffee. He sets the bag on the floor and pulls out a large textbook –
chemistry, I think. He looks up from his book
and nods at me. The world isn't what it used to be
– or is it just me?

war of the worlds

i.
The radio sits patiently in the corner
like a land mine. Waits
to deconstruct our world.

ii.
Frantic reports of disaster fill the ears of the listeners,
their eyes project the atrocity
on the walls of their living rooms.

iii.
Aliens have painted the skies red –
a deep shade of blood the sun
could only wish to compose.

iv.
Children run through the streets,
from house to house, where adults
are too afraid to open their doors.

v.
Thousands of lives lost in minutes.
Streets filled with the ashes of burning buildings,
the ashes of burning people.

vi.
We don't know who these aggressors are,
where they come from, or what they want,
because the radio doesn't know.

vii.
Eating candy and not listening to the end of the world,
our children are oblivious
to reality crumbling away like neglected teeth.

viii.
The doors are locked. Fallout shelters are stocked.
Armageddon pours from the speakers.
We are glued to the invasion of our dreams.

ix.
Bound together in the extinction of our world.
We run a three-legged race,
tied to the stones we've thrown.

x.
We wake to find the morning brilliant.
Our children are none the wiser.
The radio tricked us but we still trust it.

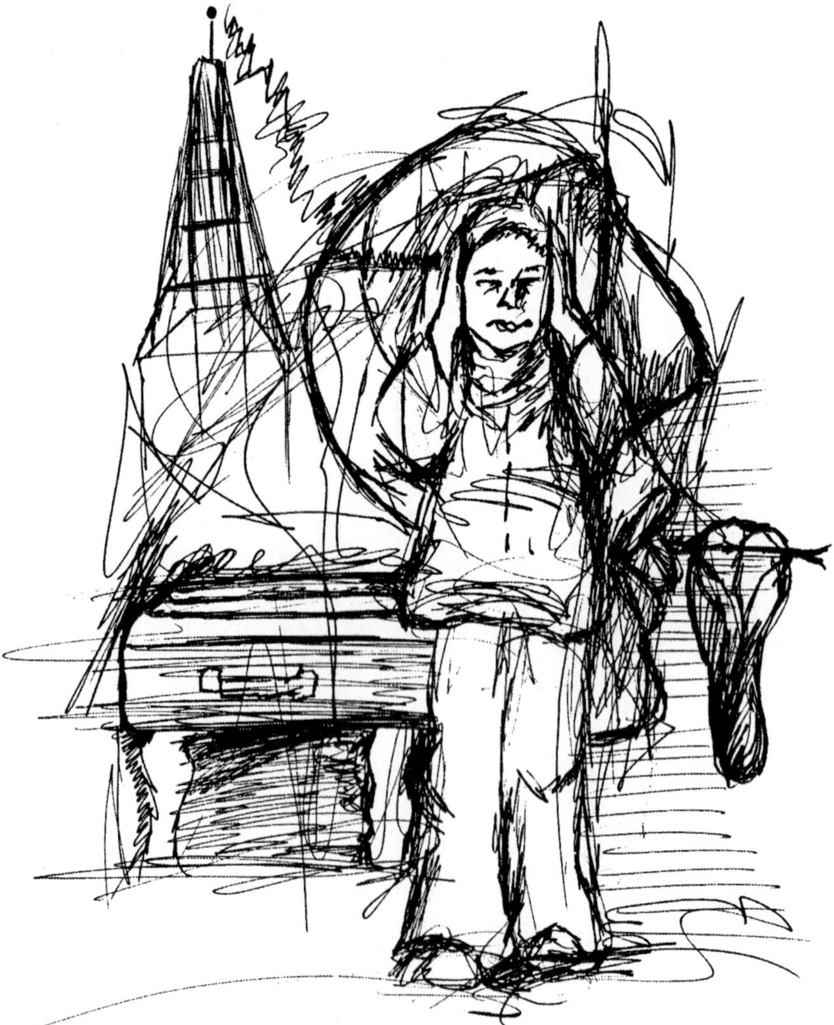

culling song
-after Chuck Palahniuk

By the end of this poem
you will be dead. Once
my words have ceased
to reverberate around the room
your ears will not be available
to hear the silence that follows.
Your ears will be petrified
trees. My words will elicit your end.
I will cause to come into being
a great death.

Upon opening the door to this room
this poem will become a contagion
and it will spread as easily as urban legends,
AIDS, or fashion trends but
the consequences will be
of nuclear proportions.
Whoever recites this poem
will be dropping bombs
from their mouth.
The poem I have composed
is constructed of mythology,
voodoo, foreign policy of a hostile nation,
nursery rhymes, wiccan chants,
and just a hint of biblical wrath.

In disbelief of the power I've culled
the local news will report a story
of a poem that kills people
upon hearing it – and in their disbelief
reporters will read this poem on the air
and their ratings will drop
by more than a margin.

Thousands of households
will be wiped out
by the evening news.
The TV station would issue
a formal apology
with coupons from a supporting restaurant
but they won't get the chance to redeem them.
This poem will go out over the wire
and other TV and radio stations
will report this poem
that supposedly kills
upon caressing the victim's ears
and how it killed
an entire viewing audience
and in turn they will lose
their listeners and viewers as well.
So you should feel privileged
to be the first victim
of my poem.

All broadcasts will cease
in fear of this poem
creeping it's way onto the air.
The people who survive the first onslaught
will retreat into a deafening fear.
All speaking will cease
just in case someone tries to kill you
with this poem. Silence
will coat the entire world like snow.

Eventually this poem will fall
into the wrong hands. Mad men
and women will use this poem
to hold their enemies hostage.
After that, evolution will do its job.

Our ears will seal up –
our heads will become unsinkable ships.
Sound will become obsolete
and we will communicate
telekinetically.

This poem's loaded chambers
will find their way into the brains
of children born 3 generations from now.
Then this poem won't even need words –
it will spread through quarantined minds
like a hungry brush fire
swallowing an entire coast,
or a computer virus
sending itself to millions of people
with the subject line,
"I love you."

After this,
we will evolve again
into a new beast –
still retreating from communicating.

hardware saint

i.
As she stands on the roof, the Virgin Mary
leans on the sign that reads "Ace Hardware."

ii.
She was spotted two days ago
outside this store by a man who was purchasing
caulk for his bathtub. He was not expecting a miracle –
just a less-leaky tub.

iii.
Accidents are piling up in the parking lot like unanswered prayers.
Surely if she stopped by once – then she'll return sometime
soon. A miracle happened in this parking lot two days ago
and that's as close as most of these people will ever get
to the residue of something that could or could not have been
great.

iv.
"I can't leave," an elderly woman with eyes like empty jewelry boxes
states when asked why she is sitting in the Ace Hardware parking lot.
"I'll stay here as long as it takes. I need
for her to come back."

v.
Inside the store, paints, nails, and circular saws are on special,
and to the disappointment of the owner, no one is buying anything.
Those people outside have till tomorrow night to see whatever it is
they're going to see, then he's going to call the cops.

it's not in me

Even if I tried
my mouth wouldn't have the significance
of a yield sign.
The abandon being displayed shows no regard
for deliberation or my outstretched hand.
You will carve a void not just inside you
but inside me and between us.
When you walk back through that door
you will be alone in every sense of the word.

Like trying to sell me a car
or switch my long distance,
you told me the situation, how it came to be
and what course of action you would be taking.
It takes three to make a crowd, two to tango,
and one finger to dial a phone and
cancel the whole thing.
If you were to listen for one second
I would tell you that the consequences
do not reside solely under your skin
but it's not in me –
it's in you.
And you are in charge.

The eyes that should have been mine,
the mouth that would have been yours
seep from the sieve of a memory
that I don't even have. That mouth will never smile,
it will never exist. But it talks to me.
Sometimes it tells me that you are right
and it will return later
for the kisses it deserves.
Most of the time that mouth
screams at me like burning churches.

Not even ashes will be left behind.
No missing persons report will be filed.

Can someone who never set foot on this earth
still have a ghost? You and I
are a defaced painting now.
When you walk back through that door
you will have revised your body for the better
and I will be unaltered.

Your soul doubled in an instant
and I missed it. Only you
can caress the void inside you –
I can simply run my hand
down your back.
I would tell you all this,
but it's not in me,
it's in you.

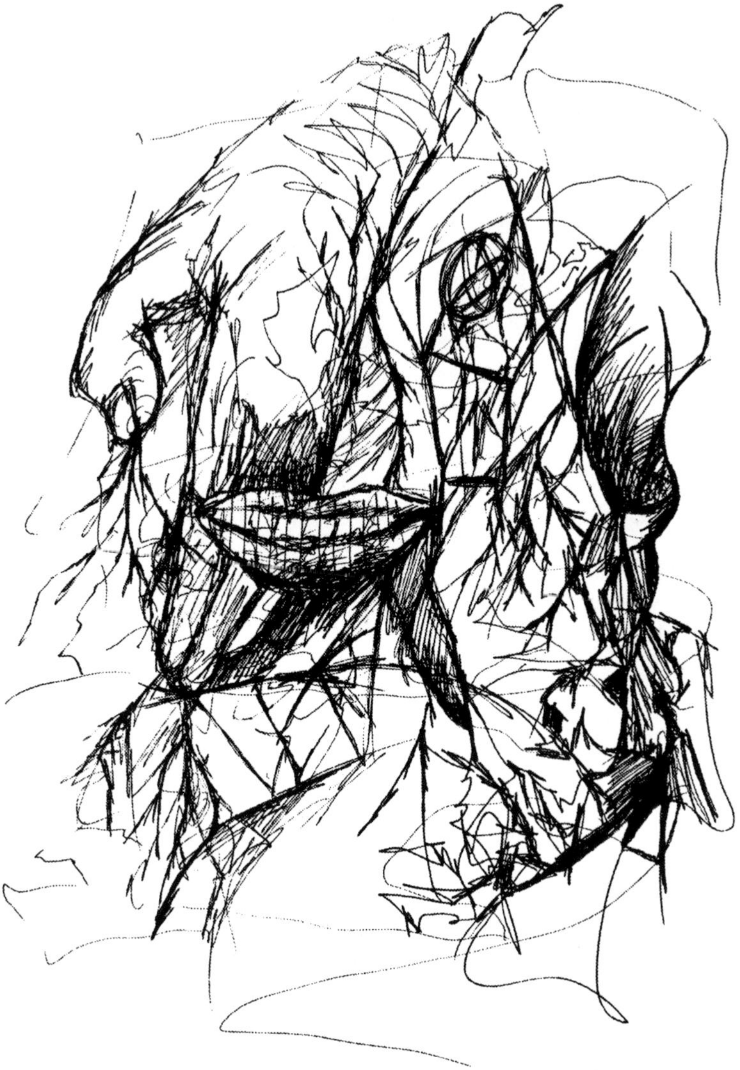

shortening of days

The vice doesn't seem so bad
at first: a sliver in my comfort,
a cold tile floor
under my hot feet.

Pupils need 43 seconds
to fully dilate. They stay
that way all season.
My eyes gasp for light.

I wake on a dark morning
to find the vice closer
to shutting completely.
Smother in evening.

The frozen teeth of icicles
sink into my body.
Slow shortening of days isn't noticed
until the sun rising is the sun setting.

Flesh is disregarded.
I am the outline of a shadow,
a footprint left in snow.
No cure other than daylight.

Barter for daylight
as if it were mine to collect.
Plead with the day
extinguishing itself.

Morning becomes evening
as I lose the space in which I live my life.
The sun is broken into white flakes descending
in a long cold dream. I will wake to blossoms.

drowning the ocean

Their marching is hushed like whispers
or rumors. The synchronized stomping of feet
sounds like thousands of clocks ticking toward
a moment of silence. The soldiers are pawns in a war
much like watches can't run backwards.
Ordered to march, so the soldiers march
until they are told to halt but that order
never comes. They march all the way to ocean cliffs
where they drop off like seconds lost in sleep.
All they have been told is the ocean is
a problem long unresolved.
Even before they take that first step in unison
their uniforms are empty.
Armed hollow shells of soldiers marching
toward the sea like days are powerless
to not follow each other toward the apocalypse.
No heads sprouting from the collars,
no fists clinched at the end of sleeves means
no hands to shake, no faces to remember.
Point them in the direction of those cliffs,
wait for the sound of the waves to dissipate
as the soldiers fill the ocean.
Wait until this solution is no longer
the desired variable
but the new constant that needs solved.
Wait until you can't tell who is winning –
when you can't discern quiet marching
from waves breaking against rocks –
when they are the same thing.

balancing cracked scales

I have a gun.
It's loaded but not for long.
I'm not going to rob some liquor store
or car-jack somebody – at least not
somebody I don't know.
I don't believe in random acts of violence.
I believe in deliberate revenge.
No harm will come to anyone
who has never harmed me.
The karmic system of checks and balances
is broken like a fifty-cent ride
outside a drug store
so I'm taking matters into my own hands –
actually, I'm letting the object in my hands
do my talking and setting straight of things.

I have a gun.
I almost feel sorry for everyone
who's going to fall prey
to their own indiscretions –
but not sorry enough not to pull
the trigger. All my memories
will be punched through with holes
as bullets zing into the carcasses
of every person, place, or thing
that has ever wronged me.
All-encompassing revenge is a daunting task
but I'm up to the challenge.
I have a long list, patience,
bullets, and I have a gun.

My entire life will fit between my crosshairs.
All my broken bones, hearts, promises,

and even broken toys will be mended
by the blood of those who have broken me.
Repeat offenders will be shot, bandaged,
and shot again until I feel justified.

Word will get around quick
that I have a gun
and I'm going to extinguish
all my smoldering crevices
by tossing carcasses on them. I will be unforgiving
and exacting. This means even my sister,
my father, and my best friend
must be felled. At one point,
each of them has crossed me
in some way. Every war
must have casualties.

I have a gun
and I will have to take revenge
on the bastard who slaughtered my family
which is me so in turn I must turn
the gun on myself. I could never shoot
myself – I don't believe in
random acts of violence or suicide.
I should hand the gun
to you. Be careful because you could
get in over your head.
Maybe I could give you a list
of the people in need of shooting
and you could do with it
what you please.

I didn't think you'd turn
the gun on me.
I guess the decision
is yours now.

men of the cloth

They are not stunned birds,
victims of invisible window panes.
They are not auto accidents
where the world takes seconds to change.
Their loss is slow like autumn
slipping away in handfuls of leaves.
Abandoning skies they have yet to navigate
for a world that left them behind.
They leave by the thousands
in a mass exodus to the middle of the street
where they stand in rush hour traffic.
They burn the house down,
tell the homeless it's made of promises
hollow as bird bones.
Only silent doves
and skeletal building frames remain
where fountains once flowed with no water
but the hope of water.

how sorry he is

He shakes my hand
and tells me how sorry he is
for my loss.
With his rusted voice he tells me
that he's known my grandfather for years.
I've never seen this man before.
Between shaky breaths he tells me
that my grandfather has a wonderful family.
So many children and grandchildren
and great-grandchildren
and they all have such illuminated faces,
even in times like these. When I tell him
that people have driven from across the country
to be here, he finally lets go of my hand
and places it against his pursed lips.
Such a loved man, he tells me, will never be gone —
look at how he lives in every face in this room.
He walks away from me and past the casket.
His clothes are creased with inattentiveness,
lacking the extra pair of eyes to recognize
that his suit is wrinkled.
The old man looks at my grandfather
lying in the coffin like he is looking
at the last square inch of earth
that has yet to be treaded upon.
His hand hovers around his trembling mouth.
As the old man walks out of the room
he shakes my hand again.
His fingers turn into wet leaves.
They cling to me.

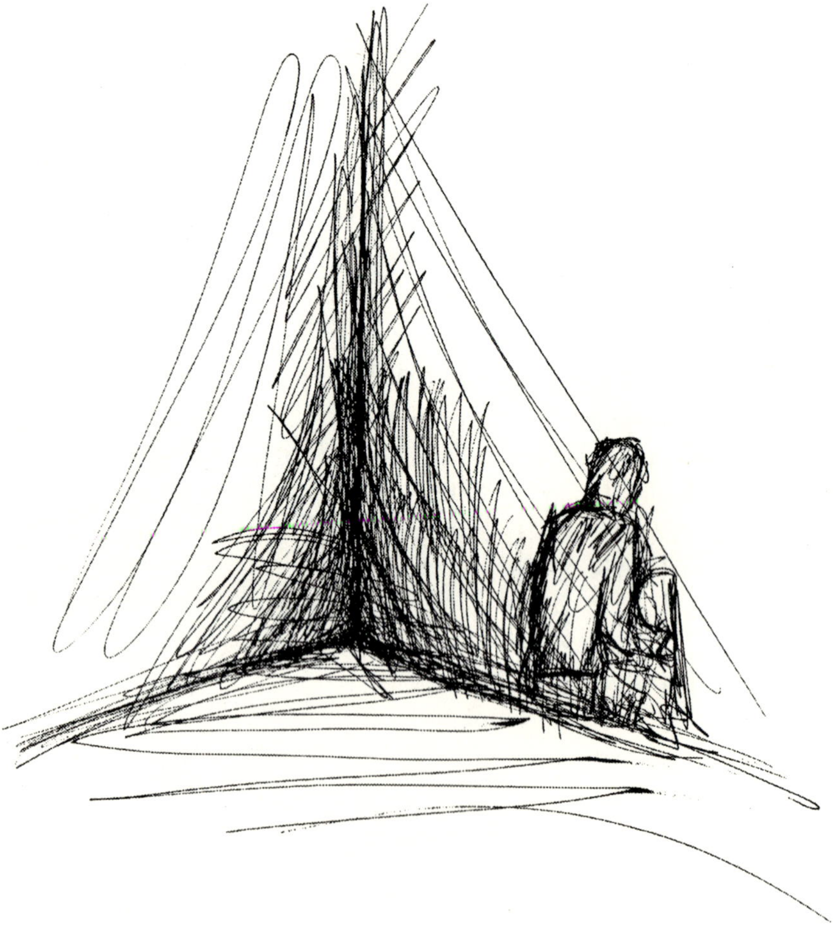

replacing our bodies

Tonight, evolution is not sufficient.
We cannot wait to be
worn away like stones in a river.
This planet we inhabit is slow –
nature bides its time
but we are not nature.
The world we live in
moves at a missile's pace
so I am not going to sit here
and not be allowed to love you
just because of who we happen to be
today. If we cannot love ourselves right now,
then we will not be ourselves.

Here is the knife. I have sharpened it
myself. The pain will be precise to the incision.

With your initial slit
peel back the epidermis.
Below this you find
the veins and arteries
where your secrets hide –
upon opening your skin
you turn into a fountain.
Your blood turns red as it exits
your body as if it's breathing
for the first time.
Continue digging and you discover
your guts – secretly inhabited like soil.
Scoop out your heart
as if you are cleaning a fish.

Hang it all on the spit
over the fire.

I do not see the details
in the murky bonfire light
as you pull yourself from yourself.
I have my knife poised as well,
pointed at my chest, ready to thrust.
Don't rush – this ceremony of liberation
and alteration, this celebration of
self-inflicted wounds, will take all night.

Once you are hollow as a cavern,
you slowly fill with echoes.
These echoes do not come from without
but from within. Deep inside you
are voices that cannot be heard
unless you give them caverns to grow louder.
Your expanding echoes sound
like they are addressing themselves –
as if they are shouting questions
that are quietly answered
with the same exact words.

When the sun rises tomorrow
we will dance in foreign flesh.
Our caresses will be those of strangers.
We will speak in a language
never heard by our ears.
Our own mouths will be our teachers,
showing us how to converse and kiss.
We will sing with the voices of the dead.
Our voices will discover a harmony so perfect
it will sound like silence.
Once we are not ourselves, we will love
like we've always wanted to love.

autumnal equinox

Leaves descend in pagan dances
as she talks with me tonight.
The trees take naked stances.
Leaves descend in pagan dances.
Only mystical influences could forge these chances.
The leaves aren't just falling – they're taking flight.
Leaves descend in pagan dances
as she talks with me tonight.

aftermath

The impact will not leave a crater.
The ridge of the skin just kissed,
a flaming ring that smolders
like city streets after a riot.
Her mouth is London
burning, spreading
as though water has never been discovered.
Lost in the streets of this moment,
I lie down in a papier-mâché museum
that surrenders its artifacts
for a new history.

Notes

we touch like cripples: The title of this poem was taken from Sylvia Plath's poem "Event."

the composer steps into the fire: This poem is a response to "The Kiss" by Anne Sexton.

a box of maniacs: The title of this poem was taken from Sylvia Plath's poem "The Arrival of the Bee Box."

ready were the almanacs: Every other line of this poem (beginning with the first line) was taken from Mike Kadela's book ***1 hundred hiccups.***

culling song: The inspiration for this poem sprang from Chuck Palahniuk's book ***Lullaby.***

Debts

Joseph kindly thanks the editors of these magazines where a number of these poems (in various stages of completion) first appeared:

Bathtub Gin
Stray Dog
Eclipse
Stirring
Poetry Motel

About the Author

Joseph Kerschbaum has performed his poetry at numerous venues around the country. He has been a featured performer at festivals such as the Bucktown Arts Fest, the Etheridge Knight Festival of the Arts, as well as Heartland Incantations, a reading series that celebrates Hoosier poets. Joseph is a member of the Bloomington Pie Cutters, a team of poets that competes within the Midwest Poetry Slam League as well as the Rustbelt Regional Poetry Slam. Joseph is also a member of the poetry troupe **Stendhal's Syndrome** with fellow poets Tony Brewer, Jenfish Superstar and Jason Ammerman. In October, 2002, Joseph released his first full-length collection of poems, ***The Human Remains***. In August, 2003, he released his first spoken word CD, ***1 of 29***. ***The Composer Steps into the Fire*** is Joseph's second full-length collection of poems.

For contact and booking information please contact the publisher or visit: **http://joseph.matrixmag.com**

About the Illustrator

Nicole Yalowitz is a Junior at Herron School of Art and Design in Indianapolis. Nicole is majoring in General Fine Arts. Her concentrations are in painting and drawing. Nicole would like to thank her husband Joel for his dedication and unwavering support.

Acknowledgements

A sincere thank you to everyone directly involved with this project. The people who tilled the soil and got their hands dirty are: Nicole Yalowitz (illustrations), Anthony Reed (cover illustration), Tony Brewer (editing), Kelly Rockhill (editing), and Akram Ibrahim (production and publication).

As far as thanking people for their kind support, humor, honesty, couches and futons, and friendship, I'm afraid there are too many of you to list. And I have too much to say about all of you. I could write an entire book to try and describe how much you all mean to me (perhaps that will be my next project). As I've said before – you know who you are.
Thank you, sincerely.

Printed in the United States
22524LVS00005B/217-219